Your Health and Wealth

A Guide to Financial and Personal Information:
What You Need to Do and Know
Before Your Spouse/Partner Dies

Lee Buchanan

BALBOA.
PRESS
A DIVISION OF HAY HOUSE

Balboa Press books may be ordered through booksellers or by contacting:

Balboa Press
A Division of Hay House
1663 Liberty Drive
Bloomington, IN 47403
www.balboapress.com
1 (877) 407-4847

Printed in the United States of America

ISBN: 978-1-4525-8271-9 (sc)

Balboa Press rev. date: 10/08/2013

To my beloved husband

Robert "Buck" Buchanan

Contents

*Sometimes an emotional moment
in the midst of
documents and dollar signs
can open doors.*
Rosemary Williams[*]

A FUNNY thing happened to me on the way to writing a book about the amazing journey of recovering from grief and loss after the death of my husband. I wrote this little book first.

As I talked with people about what I thought would be my first book, I realized that *everyone has a story* about what happened, or what didn't happen, because their loved one who died had done no planning or made no provision other than perhaps a will.

So many of us put off taking care of "final things" or making known our "end-of-life wishes" until we are "older" or until our spouse/ partner dies. We say, "I'll take care of it later."

Then when *later* comes, we are too foggy-minded by shock and grief to deal with these matters clearly and intelligently.

So, whether you are a 20-something, 30-, 40-, 50-something or older; whether you are currently single, partnered, married, separated or divorced – NOW is the time to get started documenting the information that you or others will need to know when *that time* comes. You can always add to it or make changes as your life progresses; it doesn't have to be completed in one sitting.

So, congratulations to you, reader, for taking time NOW to address some of the practical matters and the emotions/experiences that are part and parcel of the death of a spouse/partner and preparing for your own.
In this 21st century, with the rise of single women, single moms and empowered women everywhere, it's important for women to take responsibility for our part in the financial and legacy planning for ourselves and our family. And it is just as important for men to provide for

---

[*] *A Woman's Book of Money & Spiritual Vision*, p. 110.

themselves and their loved ones.

The importance of *planning* can be illustrated by examples of people who launched into their stories when I told them I was working on this little book.

Some were upset at how their family estates had been handled – or mishandled, actually – because there had been no planning.

Some said the amount of money that ended up being owed to the government in taxes would have paid for the college education of their children, had their parents done better financial and estate planning.

One of our daughters often quotes Harley Gordon:

It's never about the money . . . until it's about the money.

The families mentioned above suffered not only the loss of their loved ones, but endured years of challenges amongst themselves about what their parents could have or should have done for the disposition of their home and other assets.

You can battle it out when "the time" comes, or you can preclude much of that grief for your spouse/partner/ significant other, siblings and descendants by filling out the information in this little book and keeping it up to date. It goes without saying that writing your Last Will and Testament is of vital importance, as are the other documents indicated below.

Communication, of course, is the most important part of planning for any event. Couples communication, marriage communication is something you and your spouse/partner/significant other need to be doing all of your life together.

In my own case, we were married on Wednesday night before Thanksgiving, but my husband would not leave for our honeymoon until the following Tuesday. Why? Because he wanted to meet with the lawyer on Monday to revise his will. I suggested waiting until we came back. But he was adamant, incredibly organized and foresight-full man that he was. For my part, I was teary-eyed; it was a very happy, romantic time and I didn't want to think about things like that.

My husband is the one who had led the way of planning for our future and initiated most of the documentation we did have in place early on in our marriage. I had been a professional woman before marriage, but it wasn't until I started my own business in the 70's and was facing the bottom line every month – people first, and then the rent and utilities, etc. – that I became more aware of what's involved in being responsible for other people's welfare. I share this story especially for those of you for whom organization is not second nature... or third or even fourth!

Perhaps you are not yet conscious of the value of having a financial wishes document, or a record of your personal financial information. Perhaps you need help with organizing personal documents or to pre-plan your funeral.

If you are single, make time to talk with yourself, gather your papers and move forward to the next section.

If you are in a relationship, I suggest that you and your loved one sit down together at a time that is comfortable and meaningful to both of you and begin to go through this book and start a dialogue on what arrangements feel right for your particular situation.

In either case, when you feel complete with your information, decide who you want to share your plans with and when it would be meaningful to do so.

Purpose and clarity are needed especially when more than one person is involved. In this day of requiring transparency, there is also a need for careful planning. It is important that both/all parties state their intentions clearly.

The second most important part is to have trusted advisors/friends with whom you (both) are comfortable, because at the time when many of these plans will need to be put into action, the grieving individual may find him/herself truly challenged.

My beloved husband passed away on July 13, 2005.

What follows are things I wish we had talked about more before his death. For instance, even though he was extremely well-organized, he really did not want to plan his funeral and when pushed, suggested I talk to his sister. We were as well prepared as possible; still, questions came up.

You have the opportunity to ask questions and find out these things *now.* Some things (Parts 1-2) deal with the financial and personal records you need to start keeping now, if you haven't already done so.

Other things (Part 3) deal with *AFTER:* the emotional/ experiential component of your loved one's death that can open the door to greater awareness and the healing which the grief process can bestow.

Grief is only one of the emotions that accompany the death of a spouse. Anger and frustration are others, all of which take a toll on your health – body, mind and spirit. Having a clear and calm mind about the practical matters covered here will help you deal with other elements of the death and help to pave the way for peace at the end of life.

This book is offered to help YOU for when "that time" comes in your life. In a word, *plan now* to get ready to die so that you can relax and start having fun the rest of your life!

Lee Buchanan
Sag Harbor, NY
July 29, 2013

Notes to User:

1. Part 1 is for you, Person 1, and all of your information, some of which may overlap with that of Person 2 (your spouse/partner/significant other).

2. Part 2 is for Person 2 (your spouse/partner/significant other) and all of his/her information, some of which may overlap with that of yours (Person 1). If it does, just write *SAME.*

3. There are Note pages at the end of Part 1 and Part 2 to write additional information if the spaces provided for an item have not been sufficient. Just make a marginal note at the relevant topic to look for more information at the end.

4. If some item does not pertain, just skip it or write N/A.

Part 1: The Facts

Person 1

Personal Information

Date: _____

Full Legal Name: _____

Social security #: _____

Location of SS card: _____

Place of birth: _____
                 City   State

                Country _____

Date of birth: _____/_____/_____

If citizen of foreign country,
date entered USA: _____/_____/_____

Date of U.S. citizenship: _____/_____/_____

Father's name: _____

Mother's name: _____

Place of marriage/
Civil union   _____

Date of marriage/
Civil union   _____/_____/_____

If widowed, date of spouse's/partner's death: _____/_____/_____

If divorced, date of divorce: _____/_____/_____

If separated, date of separation: _____/_____/_____

If a veteran, branch: _____

Dates of service: _____

Personal Information (cont'd.)

Current Address

Circle one: Year-round   Winter   Summer

1. _____
   Street (and unit #) if applicable

_____
City   State   Phone number

Circle one: Year-round   Winter   Summer

2. _____
   Street (and unit #) if applicable

_____
City   State   Phone number

Circle one: Year-round   Winter   Summer

3. _____
   Street (and unit #) if applicable

_____
City   State   Phone number

Email address (personal)

1. _____

_____
Password

2. _____

_____
Password

Person 1

Child's full name

1. _____

_____/_____/_____ _____
Date of birth   Place of birth

_____
Address   Phone number

_____
Name of other parent if different than current spouse/partner

_____
Address of that parent   Phone number

2. _____

_____/_____/_____ _____
Date of birth   Place of birth

_____
Address   Phone number

_____
Name of other parent if different than current spouse/partner

_____
Address of that parent   Phone number

3. _____

_____/_____/_____ _____
Date of birth   Place of birth

_____
Address   Phone number

_____
Name of other parent if different than current spouse/partner

_____
Address of that parent   Phone number

Personal Information (cont'd.)

4. _____

_____/_____/_____ _____
Date of birth   Place of birth

_____
Address   Phone number

_____
Name of other parent if different than current spouse/partner

_____
Address of that parent   Phone number

5. _____

_____/_____/_____ _____
Date of birth   Place of birth

_____
Address   Phone number

_____
Name of other parent if different than current spouse/partner

_____
Address of that parent   Phone number

Pets

1. _____
    Name   Breed

2. _____
    Name   Breed

3. _____
    Name   Breed

Pet Insurance

_____
Company   Contact   Phone number

Person 1

Dependent Parents

Mother's full name

_____

_____/_____/_____   _____
Date of birth   Place of birth

_____
Address   Phone number

Father's full name

_____

_____/_____/_____   _____
Date of birth   Place of birth

_____
Address   Phone number

Key Contacts

Emergency Contact for
dependent children:

_____
Name   Phone number

_____
Address

Provision for their adoption if
both parents decease at the same time:

_____
Name   Phone number

_____
Address

Key Contacts (cont'd.)

Emergency Contact
for pet(s):

_____
Name

Veterinarian
(traditional): _____
                 Name   Phone number

Veterinarian
(holistic):   _____
                 Name   Phone number

Provision for adoption if
caregivers decease at the same time:

_____
Name

_____
Phone number

_____
Address

Emergency Contact for
dependent mother:

_____
Name

_____
Phone number

_____
Address

Emergency Contact for
dependent father:

_____
Name

_____
Phone number

_____
Address

Person 1

Financial
Advisor: _____
         Name   Phone number

_____
Address

Financial
Advisor: _____
         Name   Phone number

_____
Address

Accountant: _____
            Name   Phone number

_____
Address

Attorney: _____
          Name   Phone number

_____
Address

Banker: _____
        Name   Phone number

_____
Address

Physician: _____
           Name   Phone number

_____
Address

Specialist _____
           Name   Phone number

_____
Address

Key Contacts (cont'd.)

Life insurance
Agent: _____
        Name   Phone number

_____
        Address

Property and
Casualty agent: _____
        Name   Phone number

_____
        Address

Other: _____
        Name   Phone number

_____
        Address

Memberships

Boards

_____
Name   Position

_____
Contact   Phone number

_____
Name   Position

_____
Contact   Phone number

Unions

_____
Name   Position

_____
Contact   Phone number

Person 1

Name   Position

Contact   Phone number

Associations

Name   Position

Contact   Phone number

Name

Contact   Phone number

Guilds

Name   Position

Contact   Phone number

Name   Position

Contact   Phone number

Clubs

Name   Position

Contact   Phone number

Name   Position

Memberships (cont'd.)

Contact   Phone number

Financial Information

Sources of Income

Employer Company   City and State

Contact   Phone number

Email address

Password

Employer Company   City and State

Contact   Phone number

Email address

Password

Employed as 1099 subcontractor Company   City and State

Contact   Phone number

Contact   Phone number

Employed as 1099 subcontractor Company   City and State

Contact   Phone number

Self-employed Company   City and State

EIN   Phone number

Email address

Password

Self-employed Company   City and State

EIN   Phone number

Email address

Password

Pension Company   Phone number

Pension Company   Phone number

Alimony Name   Phone number

Child Support Name   Phone number

Child Support Name   Phone number

Financial Information (cont'd.)

Personal Accounts (Checking, Savings, Money Market, CDs, etc.)

Institution   Type of Account   Account number

Contact   Phone number

Institution   Type of Account   Account number

Contact   Phone number

Institution   Type of Account   Account number

Contact   Phone number

Institution   Type of Account   Account number

Contact   Phone number

Investment Accounts (brokerage, IRA, trust, etc.)

Institution   Type of Account   Account number

Contact   Phone number

Institution   Type of Account   Account number

Contact   Phone number

Institution   Type of Account   Account number

Contact		Phone number	
Institution	Type of Account	Account number	
Contact		Phone number	
Institution	Type of Account	Account number	
Contact		Phone number	

Retirement Accounts (pension, 401(k), IRA, SEP, Keogh, Annuities, etc.)

Institution	Type of Account	Account number
Contact		Phone number
Institution	Type of Account	Account number
Contact		Phone number
Institution	Type of Account	Account number
Contact		Phone number
Institution	Type of Account	Account number
Contact		Phone number
Institution	Type of Account	Account number

Financial Information (cont'd.)

_____

Contact   Phone number

For a family-owned business

_____

Owner   Name of company

_____

Address and phone number

_____

Type of corporation (Individual/sole proprietor, Corporation, Partnership, Limited Liability Company, Other)

_____

Co-owner   Phone number

_____

Co-owner   Phone number

_____

Co-owner   Phone number

_____

Co-owner   Phone number

_____

Line of succession: Name   Phone number

Life Insurance policy
owned by company
on the owner/
major officer: _____

              Institution   Policy number

Notes payable to you

_____

Name   Phone number

_____

Name   Phone number

Person 1

_____

Name   Phone number

Foreign Assets

Banking/Investments

1. _____
   Institution   Country

_____

Type of account   Account number

_____

Security information

_____

Address/Contact   Phone number

2. _____
   Institution   Country

_____

Type of account   Account number

_____

Security information

_____

Address/Contact   Phone number

3. _____
Institution   Country

_____

Type of account   Account number

_____

Security information

_____

Address/Contact   Phone number

Financial Information (cont'd.)

Property

1. _____
   Type of property (home, business, land)   Address

_____
Country   Phone number

2. _____
   Type of property (home, business, land)   Address

_____
Country   Phone number

3. _____
   Type of property (home, business, land)   Address

_____
Country   Phone number

Liabilities

Housing

__ Rent   __ Mortgage
payment to:

_____
Company or Bank/branch Location

_____
Company or Bank/branch Location

Home Equity
Line of credit _____
                Institution   Phone number

Reverse
Mortgage _____
            Institution   Phone number

Tuition

College _____
          Name   Location

Person 1

_____
      Contact   Phone number

Graduate
School _____
       Name   Location

_____
      Contact   Phone number

Loans outstanding/Notes payable

Student: _____
      Institution   Phone number

Business: _____
      Institution   Phone number

Car: _____
      Institution   Phone number

Car: _____
      Institution   Phone number

Other: _____
      Institution   Phone number

Credit Cards
(If a store card, include name)

1. _____
   Type of card   Card number   Security number

_____
New card number (if applicable)   Reason for change

2. _____
   Type of card   Card number   Security number

_____
New card number (if applicable)   Reason for change

3. _____
   Type of card   Card number   Security number

Financial Information (cont'd.)

_____
New card number (if applicable)   Reason for change

4. _____

    Type of card   Card number   Security number

_____
New card number (if applicable)   Reason for change

5. _____
    Type of card   Card number   Security number

_____
New card number (if applicable)   Reason for change

6. _____
    Type of card   Card number   Security number

_____
New card number (if applicable)   Reason for change

Valuables

Real estate/
property: _____
     Location   Deed Location

    _____
     Location   Deed Location

Safety deposit
box located at: _____
     Bank/branch City

    _____
     Box Number   Location of key

    _____
     In whose name

    _____
     Bank/branch City

Person 1

_____
Box Number   Location of key

_____
In whose name

Suze Orman
box:

_____
Location

_____
Location of key

Fire-proof safe   _____
Location

_____
Combination (or name/phone number of person who knows it)

Automobiles: _____

Make	Financing/ Leasing company	Title location

Make	Financing/ Leasing company	Title location

Jewelry _____

Item	To whom

_____

Item	To whom

_____

Item	To whom

_____

Item	To whom

_____

Item	To whom

Art   _____

Item	To whom

Financial Information (cont'd.)

_____
Item   To whom

_____
Item   To whom

_____
Item   To whom

_____
Item   To whom

Collections _____
Item   To whom

_____
Item   To whom

_____
Item   To whom

_____
Item   To whom

Employment History
Current/most recent
employer: _____
Company   Location

_____
Contact   Phone Number

Group life insurance: __ Yes __ No   __ Yes __ No
                              You   Spouse/Partner/Sig. Other

Disability: __ Yes __ No   __ Yes __ No
                              You   Spouse/Partner/Sig. Other

Stock options: __ Yes __ No   __ Yes __ No
                              You   Spouse/Partner/Sig. Other

Person 1

Company	Location

Contact	Phone Number

Group life insurance: __ Yes __ No   __ Yes __ No
                       You   Spouse/Partner/Sig. Other

Disability: __ Yes __ No   __ Yes __ No
                       You   Spouse/Partner/Sig. Other

Stock options: __ Yes __ No   __ Yes __ No
                       You   Spouse/Partner/Sig. Other

Insurance

Medical/healthcare
Insurance: _____

Primary healthcare provider   Policy number

_____

Phone number

Long-term care insurance provider   Policy number

_____

Phone number

Medicare   Policy number

_____

Phone number

Medicaid Policy number

_____

Phone number

Other medical insurance provider   Policy number

Financial Information (cont'd.)

_____
Phone number

Dental
Insurance: _____
       Dental provider   Policy number

_____
Phone number

Life insurance/
V.A. benefits: _____
       Company   Policy number

      _____
       Company   Policy number

      _____
       Company   Policy number

Automobile
insurance: _____
       Company   Policy number

Automobile
insurance: _____
       Company   Policy number

Property/Renter's
insurance: _____
       Company   Policy number

Estate Planning

Attorney: _____
      Name   Phone number

Location of

Prenuptial
agreement: _____

Current Last Will
and Testament: _____

Living Will: _____

Ethical Will _____

Letter of
last instruction: _____

Personal and charitable
trust documents: _____

HIPPA agreements _____

Power of Attorney

Financial: _____
      Name   Phone number

_____
      Document location

Important nonfinancial documents

Medical: _____
      Name   Phone number

_____
      Document location

Location of

Birth certificate: _____

Passport/citizenship
papers _____

Adoption papers
(yours): _____

Important nonfinancial documents (cont'd.)

Adoption papers
(child): _____

Adoption papers
(child): _____

Marriage certificate: _____

Family death
certificates: _____

Prenuptial
agreement: _____

Divorce or separation
agreement: _____

Military discharge
papers: _____

Appraisal and inventory
of valuable items: _____

Taxes

Prior years' federal
and state returns: _____

Federal/state gift
tax returns: _____

Property and
School tax returns: _____

Small business
Incorporation/
Ownership papers: _____

Buy/sell
agreements: _____

Websites (yours)

1: _____

Name   URL

_____

Host Name   URL

_____

Location of User ID, Password & security Q&A

2: _____

Name   URL

_____

Host Name   URL

_____

Location of User ID, Password & security Q&A

3: _____

Name   URL

_____

Host Name   URL

_____

Location of User ID, Password & security Q&A

Blogs (yours)

1: _____

Name   URL

_____

Host Name   URL

_____

Location of User ID, Password & security Q&A

2: _____

Name   URL

Blogs (yours), cont'd.

_____

Host Name   URL

_____

Location of User ID, Password & security Q&A

Important Internet accounts

1: _____

Name   URL

_____

Location of password & security Q&A

2: _____

Name   URL

_____

Location of password & security Q&A

3: _____

Name   URL

_____

Location of password & security Q&A

4: _____

Name   URL

_____

Location of password & security Q&A

5: _____

Name   URL

_____

Location of password & security Q&A

6: _____

Name   URL

Location of password & security Q&A

7: _____
Name   URL

Location of password & security Q&A

8: _____
Name   URL

Location of password & security Q&A

8: _____
Name   URL

Location of password & security Q&A

10: _____
Name   URL

Important Social Network accounts

1: _____
Name   URL

Location of password & security Q&A

2: _____
Name   URL

Location of password & security Q&A

3: _____
Name   URL

Location of password & security Q&A

Important Social Network accounts (cont'd.)

4: _____

    Name   URL

_____

Location of password & security Q&A

5: _____

    Name   URL

Important information regarding serious illness or death

Home health care
provider: _____

    Name   Location

_____

    Contact   Phone number

Nursing home/
Assisted living: _____

    Name   Location

_____

    Contact   Phone number

Hospice: _____

    Name   Location

_____

    Contact   Phone number

Church/temple: _____

    Name   Phone number

_____

    Contact   Phone number

Person 1

Personal contacts:
In addition to the professional persons named to this point, please notify the following:

FAMILY (also indicate who is Next of Kin)

Relationship	Name	Phone number

Relationship	Name	Phone number

Relationship	Name	Phone number

Relationship	Name	Phone number

Relationship	Name	Phone number

Relationship	Name	Phone number

FRIENDS

Name	Phone number

Name	Phone number

Name	Phone number

Name	Phone number

Name	Phone number

Name	Phone number

Important information regarding serious illness or death (cont'd.)

BUSINESS COLLEAGUES

Company	Name	Phone number

Company	Name	Phone number

Company	Name	Phone number

Company	Name	Phone number

Company	Name	Phone number

Company	Name	Phone number

NEIGHBORS

Name	Phone number

Name	Phone number

Name	Phone number

Name	Phone number

Name	Phone number

Name	Phone number

Funeral, Memorial Service, Burial

I have made funeral
arrangements with: _____

                    Name

_____

                    Address

_____

                    Contact   Phone number

Burial plot
arrangements: _____

               Name

_____

              Address

_____

              Contact   Phone number

I have not made arrangements,
but would like the following:

Location of
Wake: ___None ___ At home ___ Church ___ Funeral home

_____

           Preferred funeral home   Phone number

_____

           Address

_____

           Type of arrangements (burial/cremation)

_____

           Cemetery   Location

If planning a
cremation, what
is your preference
for the remains? _____

Important information regarding serious illness or death (cont'd.)

_____

_____

_____

Information I would
like included in
my obituary: _____

_____

_____

_____

_____

_____

No obituary ___

Flowers
Flowers for the wake ___ Yes ___ No

Flowers for the funeral/
memorial service ___ Yes ___ No

No flowers at all ___

In lieu of flowers,
preferred memorial
donations: _____

_____

_____

Food and drink afterward

___None   ___ At home   ___ Restaurant (see below)

Restaurant: _____

         Name   Phone number

_____

         Address

Notes *(for any additional information)*

_____

_____

_____

_____

_____

_____

_____

_____

_____

_____

_____

_____

_____

_____

_____

_____

_____

Person 1

Person 1

Part 2: The Facts
Person 2
(Spouse/Partner/Significant Other)

Personal Information

Date: _____

Full Legal Name: _____

Social security #: _____

Location of SS card: _____

Place of birth: _____
                City   State

                       Country _____

Date of birth: _____/_____/_____

If citizen of foreign country,
date entered USA: _____/_____/_____

Date of U.S. citizenship: _____/_____/_____

Father's name: _____

Mother's name: _____

Place of marriage/
Civil union   _____

Date of marriage/
Civil union   _____/_____/_____

If widowed, date of spouse's/partner's death: _____/_____/_____

If divorced, date of divorce: _____/_____/_____

If separated, date of separation: _____/_____/_____

If a veteran, branch: _____

Dates of service: _____

Personal Information (cont'd.)

Current Address

Circle one: Year-round   Winter   Summer

1. _____
   Street (and unit #) if applicable

_____
City   State   Phone number

Circle one: Year-round   Winter   Summer

2. _____
   Street (and unit #) if applicable

_____
City   State   Phone number

Circle one: Year-round   Winter   Summer

3. _____
   Street (and unit #) if applicable

_____
City   State   Phone number

Email address (personal)

1. _____

_____
Password

2. _____

_____
Password

Person 2

Child's full name

1. _____

_____/_____/_____ _____
Date of birth   Place of birth

_____
Address   Phone number

_____
Name of other parent if different than current spouse/partner

_____
Address of that parent   Phone number

2. _____

_____/_____/_____ _____
Date of birth   Place of birth

_____
Address   Phone number

_____
Name of other parent if different than current spouse/partner

_____
Address of that parent   Phone number

3. _____

_____/_____/_____ _____
Date of birth   Place of birth

_____
Address   Phone number

_____
Name of other parent if different than current spouse/partner

_____
Address of that parent   Phone number

Personal Information (cont'd.)

4. _____

_____/_____/_____ _____
Date of birth   Place of birth

_____
Address   Phone number

_____
Name of other parent if different than current spouse/partner

_____
Address of that parent   Phone number

5. _____

_____/_____/_____ _____
Date of birth   Place of birth

_____
Address   Phone number

_____
Name of other parent if different than current spouse/partner

_____
Address of that parent   Phone number

Pets

1. _____
   Name   Breed

2. _____
   Name   Breed

3. _____
   Name   Breed

Pet Insurance

_____
Company   Contact   Phone number

Dependent Parents

Mother's full name

_____

_____/_____/_____ _____
Date of birth   Place of birth

_____
Address   Phone number

Father's full name

_____

_____/_____/_____ _____
Date of birth   Place of birth

_____
Address   Phone number

Key Contacts

Emergency Contact for
dependent children:

_____
Name   Phone number

_____
Address

Provision for their adoption if
both parents decease at the same time:

_____
Name   Phone number

_____
Address

Key Contacts (cont'd.)

Emergency Contact
for pet(s):

_____

Name

Veterinarian
(traditional): _____

Name   Phone number

Veterinarian
(holistic):   _____

Name   Phone number

Provision for adoption if
caregivers decease at the same time:

_____

Name

_____

Phone number

_____

Address

Emergency Contact for
dependent mother:

_____

Name

_____

Phone number

_____

Address

Emergency Contact for
dependent father:

_____

Name

_____

Phone number

_____

Address

Person 2

Financial
Advisor: _____
        Name   Phone number

_____
        Address

Financial
Advisor: _____
        Name   Phone number

_____
        Address

Accountant: _____
        Name   Phone number

_____
        Address

Attorney: _____
        Name   Phone number

_____
        Address

Banker: _____
        Name   Phone number

_____
        Address

Physician: _____
        Name   Phone number

_____
        Address

Specialist _____
        Name   Phone number

_____
        Address

Key Contacts (cont'd.)

Life insurance
Agent: _____
 Name   Phone number

_____
 Address

Property and
Casualty agent: _____
 Name   Phone number

_____
 Address

Other: _____
 Name   Phone number

_____
 Address

Memberships

Boards

_____
Name   Position

_____
Contact   Phone number

_____
Name   Position

_____
Contact   Phone number

Unions

_____
Name   Position

_____
Contact   Phone number

Person 2

Name   Position

Contact   Phone number

Associations

Name   Position

Contact   Phone number

Name

Contact   Phone number

Guilds

Name   Position

Contact   Phone number

Name   Position

Contact   Phone number

Clubs

Name   Position

Contact   Phone number

Name   Position

Memberships (cont'd.)

Contact   Phone number

Financial Information

Sources of Income

Employer Company   City and State

Contact   Phone number

Email address

Password

Employer Company   City and State

Contact   Phone number

Email address

Password

Employed as 1099 subcontractor Company   City and State

Contact   Phone number

Contact   Phone number

Employed as 1099 subcontractor Company | City and State

Contact | Phone number

Self-employed Company | City and State

EIN | Phone number

Email address

Password

Self-employed Company | City and State

EIN | Phone number

Email address

Password

Pension Company | Phone number

Pension Company | Phone number

Alimony Name | Phone number

Child Support Name | Phone number

Child Support Name | Phone number

Financial Information (cont'd.)

Personal Accounts (Checking, Savings, Money Market, CDs, etc.)

_____

Institution   Type of Account   Account number

_____

Contact   Phone number

_____

Institution   Type of Account   Account number

_____

Contact   Phone number

_____

Institution   Type of Account   Account number

_____

Contact   Phone number

_____

Institution   Type of Account   Account number

_____

Contact   Phone number

Investment Accounts (brokerage, IRA, trust, etc.)

_____

Institution   Type of Account   Account number

_____

Contact   Phone number

_____

Institution   Type of Account   Account number

_____

Contact   Phone number

_____

Institution   Type of Account   Account number

Person 2

Contact		Phone number

Institution	Type of Account	Account number

Contact		Phone number

Institution	Type of Account	Account number

Contact		Phone number

Retirement Accounts (pension, 401(k), IRA, SEP, Keogh, Annuities, etc.)

Institution	Type of Account	Account number

Contact		Phone number

Institution	Type of Account	Account number

Contact		Phone number

Institution	Type of Account	Account number

Contact		Phone number

Institution	Type of Account	Account number

Contact		Phone number

Institution	Type of Account	Account number

Financial Information (cont'd.)

Contact   Phone number

For a family-owned business

Owner   Name of company

Address and phone number

Type of corporation (Individual/sole proprietor, Corporation, Partnership, Limited Liability Company, Other)

Co-owner   Phone number

Co-owner   Phone number

Co-owner   Phone number

Co-owner   Phone number

Line of succession: Name   Phone number

Life Insurance policy
owned by company
on the owner/
major officer: _____
               Institution   Policy number

Notes payable to you

Name   Phone number

Name   Phone number

Name   Phone number

Foreign Assets

Banking/Investments

1. _____
   Institution   Country

_____
Type of account   Account number

_____
Security information

_____
Address/Contact   Phone number

2. _____
   Institution   Country

_____
Type of account   Account number

_____
Security information

_____
Address/Contact   Phone number

3. _____
Institution   Country

_____
Type of account   Account number

_____
Security information

_____
Address/Contact   Phone number

Financial Information (cont'd.)

Property

1. _____
    Type of property (home, business, land)   Address

_____
Country   Phone number

2. _____
    Type of property (home, business, land)   Address

_____
Country   Phone number

3. _____
    Type of property (home, business, land)   Address

_____
Country   Phone number

Liabilities

Housing

__ Rent   __ Mortgage

payment to:

_____
    Company or Bank/branch Location

_____
    Company or Bank/branch Location

Home Equity
Line of credit _____
        Institution   Phone number

Reverse
Mortgage _____
        Institution   Phone number

Tuition

College _____
     Name   Location

_____

Contact   Phone number

Graduate
School _____
      Name   Location

_____

    Contact   Phone number

Loans outstanding/Notes payable

Student: _____
        Institution   Phone number

Business: _____
         Institution   Phone number

Car: _____
    Institution   Phone number

Car: _____
    Institution   Phone number

Other: _____
      Institution   Phone number

Credit Cards
(If a store card, include name)

1. _____
  Type of card   Card number   Security number

_____

New card number (if applicable)   Reason for change

2. _____
  Type of card   Card number   Security number

_____

New card number (if applicable)   Reason for change

3. _____
  Type of card   Card number   Security number

Financial Information (cont'd.)

_____

New card number (if applicable)   Reason for change

4. _____

   Type of card   Card number   Security number

_____

New card number (if applicable)   Reason for change

5. _____

   Type of card   Card number   Security number

_____

New card number (if applicable)   Reason for change

6. _____

   Type of card   Card number   Security number

_____

New card number (if applicable)   Reason for change

Valuables

Real estate/
property: _____

   Location   Deed Location

_____

   Location   Deed Location

Safety deposit
box located at: _____

   Bank/branch   City

_____

   Box Number   Location of key

_____

   In whose name

_____

   Bank/branch   City

Person 2

Box Number   Location of key

In whose name

Suze Orman box:

Location

Location of key

Fire-proof safe

Location

Combination (or name/phone number of person who knows it)

Automobiles: _____

Make	Financing/ Leasing company	Title location

Make	Financing/ Leasing company	Title location

Jewelry _____

Item	To whom

Item	To whom

Item	To whom

Item	To whom

Item	To whom

Art _____

Item	To whom

Financial Information (cont'd.)

_____

Item   To whom

_____

Item   To whom

_____

Item   To whom

_____

Item   To whom

Collections _____
                 Item   To whom

_____

Item   To whom

_____

Item   To whom

_____

Item   To whom

Employment History
Current/most recent
employer: _____
          Company   Location

_____

     Contact   Phone Number

Group life insurance: __ Yes __ No   __ Yes __ No
                             You   Spouse/Partner/Sig. Other

Disability: __ Yes __ No   __ Yes __ No
                             You   Spouse/Partner/Sig. Other

Stock options: __ Yes __ No   __ Yes __ No
                             You   Spouse/Partner/Sig. Other

Person 2

Company	Location

Contact	Phone Number

Group life insurance: __ Yes __ No   __ Yes __ No
You   Spouse/Partner/Sig. Other

Disability: __ Yes __ No   __ Yes __ No
You   Spouse/Partner/Sig. Other

Stock options: __ Yes __ No   __ Yes __ No
You   Spouse/Partner/Sig. Other

Insurance
Medical/healthcare
Insurance: _____

Primary healthcare provider   Policy number

Phone number

Long-term care insurance provider   Policy number

Phone number

Medicare   Policy number

Phone number

Medicaid   Policy number

Phone number

Other medical insurance provider   Policy number

Financial Information (cont'd.)

_____
Phone number

Dental
Insurance: _____
Dental provider   Policy number

_____
Phone number

Life insurance/
V.A. benefits: _____
Company   Policy number

_____
Company   Policy number

_____
Company   Policy number

Automobile
insurance: _____
Company   Policy number

Automobile
insurance: _____
Company   Policy number

Property/Renter's
insurance: _____
Company   Policy number

Estate Planning

Attorney: _____
Name   Phone number

Location of

Prenuptial
agreement: _____

Current Last Will
and Testament: _____

Living Will: _____

Ethical Will _____

Letter of
last instruction: _____

Personal and charitable
trust documents: _____

HIPPA agreements _____

Power of Attorney

Financial: _____
      Name   Phone number

_____
      Document location

Important nonfinancial documents

Medical: _____
      Name   Phone number

_____
      Document location

Location of

Birth certificate: _____

Passport/citizenship
papers _____

Adoption papers
(yours): _____

Important nonfinancial documents (cont'd.)

Adoption papers
(child): _____

Adoption papers
(child): _____

Marriage certificate: _____

Family death
certificates: _____

Prenuptial
agreement: _____

Divorce or separation
agreement: _____

Military discharge
papers: _____

Appraisal and inventory
of valuable items: _____

Taxes

Prior years' federal
and state returns: _____

Federal/state gift
tax returns: _____

Property and
School tax returns: _____

Small business
Incorporation/
Ownership papers: _____

Buy/sell
agreements: _____

Websites (yours)

1: _____

Name   URL

_____

Host Name   URL

_____

Location of User ID, Password & security Q&A

2: _____

Name   URL

_____

Host Name   URL

_____

Location of User ID, Password & security Q&A

3: _____

Name   URL

_____

Host Name   URL

_____

Location of User ID, Password & security Q&A

Blogs (yours)

1: _____

Name   URL

_____

Host Name   URL

_____

Location of User ID, Password & security Q&A

2: _____

Name   URL

Blogs (yours), cont'd.

_____

Host Name   URL

_____

Location of User ID, Password & security Q&A

Important Internet accounts

1: _____

Name   URL

_____

Location of password & security Q&A

2: _____

Name   URL

_____

Location of password & security Q&A

3: _____

Name   URL

_____

Location of password & security Q&A

4: _____

Name   URL

_____

Location of password & security Q&A

5: _____

Name   URL

_____

Location of password & security Q&A

6: _____

Name   URL

Location of password & security Q&A

7: _____
    Name   URL

Location of password & security Q&A

8: _____
    Name   URL

Location of password & security Q&A

8: _____
    Name   URL

Location of password & security Q&A

10: _____
    Name   URL

Important Social Network accounts

1: _____
    Name   URL

Location of password & security Q&A

2: _____
    Name   URL

Location of password & security Q&A

3: _____
    Name   URL

Location of password & security Q&A

Important Social Network accounts (cont'd.)

4: _____
   Name   URL

_____
   Location of password & security Q&A

5: _____
   Name   URL

Important information regarding serious illness or death

Home health care
provider: _____
                Name   Location

_____
                Contact   Phone number

Nursing home/
Assisted living: _____
                Name   Location

_____
                Contact   Phone number

Hospice: _____
                Name   Location

_____
                Contact   Phone number

Church/temple: _____
                Name   Phone number

_____
                Contact   Phone number

Personal contacts:

*In addition to the professional persons named to this point,
please notify the following:*

FAMILY (also indicate who is Next of Kin)

Relationship	Name	Phone number
Relationship	Name	Phone number
Relationship	Name	Phone number
Relationship	Name	Phone number
Relationship	Name	Phone number
Relationship	Name	Phone number

FRIENDS

Name	Phone number
Name	Phone number
Name	Phone number
Name	Phone number
Name	Phone number
Name	Phone number

Important information regarding serious illness or death (cont'd.)

BUSINESS COLLEAGUES

Company	Name	Phone number

Company	Name	Phone number

Company	Name	Phone number

Company	Name	Phone number

Company	Name	Phone number

Company	Name	Phone number

NEIGHBORS

Name	Phone number

Name	Phone number

Name	Phone number

Name	Phone number

Name	Phone number

Name	Phone number

Funeral, Memorial Service, Burial

I have made funeral
arrangements with: _____
 Name

_____

 Address

_____

 Contact   Phone number

Burial plot
arrangements: _____
 Name

_____

 Address

_____

 Contact   Phone number

I have not made arrangements,
but would like the following:

Location of
Wake: ___None ___ At home ___ Church ___ Funeral home

_____

 Preferred funeral home   Phone number

_____

 Address

_____

 Type of arrangements (burial/cremation)

_____

 Cemetery   Location

If planning a
cremation, what
is your preference
for the remains? _____

Important information regarding serious illness or death (cont'd.)

_____

_____

_____

Information I would
like included in
my obituary: _____

_____

_____

_____

_____

_____

No obituary ___

Flowers
Flowers for the wake ___ Yes ___ No

Flowers for the funeral/
memorial service   ___ Yes ___ No

No flowers at all ___

In lieu of flowers,
preferred memorial
donations: _____

_____

_____

Person 2

Food and drink afterward

___None   ___ At home   ___ Restaurant (see below)

Restaurant: _____
          Name   Phone number

      _____
          Address

Notes *(for any additional information)*

Person 2

Person 2

Part 3: The Emotions and Experiences

I F you have taken the time earlier in your life to fill out the preceding pages and keep them updated, then you will be relieved of that huge organizational burden adding to the complexity of all the human, relational, emotional, love and grieving issues that emerge at the time of someone's death.

When your loved one dies, many things may happen, many different events may occur; you may find yourself worrying or obsessing. As you process these feelings, it is important to give yourself time to feel them, to find time to be alone with them, time to just be in the feeling. In a word, *dive deeper into your heart space.* This means quieting your mind and turning your attention inward to your heart center, where you can just be still. As the psalmist says,

Be still and know that I am God.
Psalm 46:10

Grief is the price you pay for love. It comes in many forms, often carefully wrapped, packaged and labeled with a variety of confusing names. Depression and anxiety are two of the more common ones. This can create additional problems. However, grief, when it is honored, understood and guided, can aid in the healing process. This can be helped by having a trusted and understanding loved one or friend to just talk to. One who can listen without feeling the need to step in and help. At times there may be no professional help, such as a therapist or grief specialist, readily available.

Awareness of the following topics will help you honor yourself and your loved one so that you may have peace at the end of life.

Emotions. Dealing with all the emotions that come up at the time of death can be overwhelming. Men frequently process grief differently than women. Crying is what we do most likely, when we can't or perhaps don't know what else to do. It is important to let the tears flow. Do not keep them permanently parked just below the surface. Allow them to flow at their own will and pace. Tears are also a way of processing the hurt, the pain, the regrets, the disappointments and the questions that arise at this and many other times.

Also, it is important to acknowledge feelings of anger; these feelings may or may not be aided by crying. Anger can arise for any number of reasons, including the cause of death. Again it is important how we process these feelings. As we slog through these emotions, we must also allow for the memories of the love, the joy, the laughter and the good times.

At the time of my husband's passing, I allowed the tears; *hysteria* is a better word. Then spent years feeling embarrassed by my own behavior. It wasn't as though his passing was unexpected. After years of illness, he had just spent days in the hospital with a couple of touch-and-go situations. When his doctor came to the house to pronounce and set the time of passing, he said, "He wanted to come home to die." I believe that. I also believe he waited for his sister to arrive before he passed.

With the passing of a loved one and the next steps to be taken, one may be feeling the old saying, "Ours is not to reason why, ours is but to do or die," so one begins to move forward with planning, but at times with the feeling of driving on a two-lane highway in the fog. There will be time to address all the emotions in the days, weeks and months – even years – to come. Right now, however, you will need all the strength you can muster to take care of the situation at hand.

Funerals. Rituals are important, be they religious or otherwise. Shiva is the week-long mourning period in Judaism for first-degree relatives. In other traditions funerals of some sort or a memorial service are an expected part of dying. They are, I believe, meant to provide an opportunity for those involved to allow a release of feelings and to commemorate the life of our loved ones and a life lived. At their best, they are most likely planned in advance according to one's beliefs and special requests.

Sometimes a death occurs where there has been no planning. Some of us, perhaps, try to protect ourselves by not thinking about it. At times such as these, family and loved ones can be most helpful. Also seek out the help of your local pastor, priest or rabbi, or a respected person from whom you may have previously sought advice.

Finances. When we plan for carrying on our life after our spouse/ partner dies, finances are an essential part of the planning. It is unfortunate that they have to be dealt with when we are in our most vulnerable state. How we feel and what we do with our money is often an issue. All the more reason to have planned finances and other such matters in advance. Talk openly with each other; consult with professionals about estate planning and legacy planning.

Time to process feelings. The feeling of isolation or even isolating ourselves may begin to appear. At times we may feel the need to be alone to deal with our pain.

Pain is the breaking of the shell
that encloses your understanding.
Kahlil Gibran, *The Prophet*

At times we need rest. At times we need the warmth and presence of our loved ones.

Prayer and meditation. These spiritual practices helped me and countless others. I have read that prayer is talking to God and meditation is listening to God. I have also read that prayer connects us with the cosmos. Wasn't it Frank Sinatra who said, "I'm for anything that gets you through the night"?

Health. Grief is often misunderstood because it has such complex components. It is a vulnerable time and it is not uncommon to receive well-meant suggestions for various medications, which may or may not help you feel better. Your health – always, but especially when grieving – is very important. Take care of yourself, first and foremost.

Sleep and dreams. Sleep is an important commodity always, but especially during times of deep and abiding grief. Dreams are partners with sleep – at times comforting and at times disturbing; and at times we find ourselves questioning them, with logic coming up missing. A dream may feel like a sign from a loved one or loved ones; just allow. If you can, write down your dreams as soon as you remember them.

Grief support. Should you find yourself feeling the need to repeat your story over and over, you may be searching for answers. It is important to have someone to talk to or with about your grief and loss. Again there are people and organizations especially designed to help. Find one that is comfortable for you. Remember it is YOUR story. The subject may be universal, but your story is unique. Living your story may have created the feelings, but it is also living your story that will lead you to answers.

Writing. This may also be a good time, if you have not done it before, to start writing. Writing can be one of the most enlightening activities that presently exist for dealing with the challenges of emotions and experiences. Journaling or letter writing can be most effective. Write to the person with whom you would wish to communicate, living or departed. Feel free to then send it, burn it or just simply put it away to read later.

The important thing is to express your feelings, whether they are questions, opinions or stories – happy, sad, angry – or just to record that you are here today and breathing. The act of writing can be healing. Feel free to write yourself an answer to any of them. This, too, can be amazing.

Cleaning and clearing. As you begin the process of sorting out clothes and belongings and clearing out closets, rooms and various parts of the home, maybe even an office, remember that your loved one will not need these belongings or goods again. Honest! This is a good time to ask for help. Most people really do want to help, they just don't know when or how. As you wade through this cleaning and clearing process, you may be surprised by what may turn up. Possessions carry their own energy. This is an activity that may bring up an array of feelings and memories ranging from surprise, laughter, confusion and pain, and perhaps questions unimaginable until now.

Omission. Remember that there are many different reasons most of us do not share everything about ourselves. The reasons include not wishing to bore another, or the subject is too unimportant to remember. At other times we may feel the need to protect ourselves when something is too painful, too frightful or too embarrassing to bear repeating.

Intimacy. This is another devastating loss. Whatever the age. When two people are deeply in love, you may have wonderful memories of love making, of the times when you may have felt so alone in a situation and then being with your loved one brought you together as one. At times our need to feel loved, to feel connected to another human being, may or may not involve sex. These feelings may not be easily discussed with friends. Some may wish it were possible again right away, others may feel they couldn't even think of being involved again with another person. The role of lover/spouse/partner may not easily be reassigned.

Calendar dates. Anniversaries and holidays need planning. The anniversary of a death can be one of the most challenging. Careful planning can sometimes help alleviate the pain. It is beneficial to be with loved ones with whom you have enjoyed previous festivities. Try to remember the good ones and look for something to remind you of them.

Closure. There is a lot of advice out there concerning closure. According to the dictionary, closure is "the act of closing or the state of being closed." I have heard that the Latin source means "closing the gap between two things." For some of us, there is no such thing as closure. How we handle this subject may have a lot to do with circumstances, and has to be handled on a case-by-case basis. This is where the planning becomes so important.

Finally, as someone has said so well:

> *People may forget what you said*
> *and they may forget what you did,*
> *but they will never forget*
> *how you made them feel.*

Lee Buchanan

Moving Forward

As we witnessed the labor of new life, we would see many of the same signs that accompany the loss of life in our world.
Gregg Braden[†]

Even with solid planning in place for the event of one's passing, a lot will change along the way.

I have deliberately not included a place for names and phone numbers of service/support people who are likely to vary after you complete this document (remember to list the Poison Control number if you have children and/or pets). But you'll want and need to have a list handy near your phone or the kitchen calendar for such people that you and/or your spouse/partner deal with on a day-to-day basis for general living, but also in case of accidental death, etc., so that they may be properly notified, especially if there are outstanding appointments. For instance:

- Dentist
- Doctor
- Dry cleaner
- Electrician
- Hair dresser/barber
- Lawn/yard care service
- Plumber
- Veterinarian
- Visiting nurse/hospice caregiver

My husband and I had the benefit of good advice and preparation and as his life began to slip away we were able to keep self-correcting, rather like a race car driver does – and still, challenges arose that would have been almost impossible to anticipate. And some *were* impossible to anticipate.

Laws kept changing and our bank was sold, so we experienced fluctuating scenarios of trusted advisors as personnel changes were made by the new bank ownership, etc. Advisors retired and some died. In other cases,

---

[†] *Secrets of the Lost Mode of Prayer*, p. 147.

relationships were formed and then changed, but we managed to stay abreast so that at the time of my husband's death we were comfortable that plans were in place and all was well.

And yet, once he was gone, and I was operating in a foggy state of grief, I found myself with challenges for which I didn't feel prepared.

That is why I have written this little book, to help YOU through that foggy darkness to create your new life on the other side of your loved one's passing.

Now my own moving forward includes writing a book whose working title is *Journey of a Grieving Soul: Completing an Unfinished Marriage.*

LIFE IS GOOD.

Suggested Reading and Resources

American Bar Association. *Guide to Wills and Estates.* New York: Times Books, 2009.

James, John W. and Russell Friedman. *The Grief Recovery Handbook.* Sherman Oaks, CA: Grief Recovery Institute.

Kubler-Ross, Elisabeth and David Kessler. *On Grief and Grieving.* Scribner (2007)

LegalZoom.com offers a multitude of products and forms for personal and boniness needs.

Personal Financial Organizer – these can be obtained from numerous online vendors; check also with your bank.

Williams, Rosemary. *A Woman's Book of Money & Spiritual Vision,* Philadelphia, PA: Innisfree Press, Inc., 2001

Acknowledgments

A brief thank you to Buck, our daughters Heather and Holly, Lynne Walker, Blake Kerr, Dawn Sibley, Colleen Higgins, Roy Cashion and my wonderful editor Catherine who has understood not only my words, but my thoughts; and of course Ra and Fa – for without them this little book would never have materialized.

About the Author

Photo by Robin Serna

Lee Buchanan is currently a Grief Recovery Specialist trained at the Grief Recovery Institute in California. She was a professional woman in the Travel Industry, one of the first stewardesses (now flight attendants) to take to the skies in the new jet age, when she met and married her husband and became mother of twins. In the 70's she became co-owner of The Travel Store travel agency. Lee had been married almost 44 years at the time of her husband's passing.

Contact Lee at cronesnest@hotmail.com.

What readers are saying about *Your Health and Wealth*

Procrastinate *literally means "for tomorrow". Sometimes the result of putting things off is like closing the barn door after the horse has bolted. To counterbalance procrastination, the author addresses facing important end-of-life issues beforehand in a simple, straightforward manner. This little book is big on practicals—finding out and recording important personal and business information in one place...while you and your spouse or loved one are still living. If you are willing to look and plan ahead, Lee Buchanan's* Your Health and Wealth *will be a very helpful tool before and when the separation time comes. After this glimpse, I am eager to read what Lee will write in her intended book,* Journey of a Grieving Soul.

– Lizzie Magnusson

[This] really is a very beneficial book to have for any family. We have recently gone through a year of trying to find out "where everything was" for my father-in-law, who passed away a year ago. If we had had all the necessary information available, it would have saved a lot of grief

– Nelleke and Tim Oei

Lee's book is truly a gift of love. It will help all who have suffered the loss of a loved one.

– Andrew Fuller, OSB

A MUST read for anyone who wants to achieve inner peace in a dynamic and often chaotic world. Lee gives you everything you need to know and do to prepare for one of life's greatest uncertainties – the death of a loved one.

– International best-selling author, Tim Connor